SCHIRMER'S LIBRARY
OF MUSICAL CLASSICS

Vol 444

GIOVANNI BATTISTA VIOTTI

Concerto No. 23
IN G MAJOR
FOR
VIOLIN

With accompaniment of
ORCHESTRA

———

Revised after the edition of
FERDINAND DAVID
By
HENRY SCHRADIECK

ISBN 978-0-7935-5676-2

G. SCHIRMER, Inc.

DISTRIBUTED BY
HAL•LEONARD®
CORPORATION
7777 W. BLUEMOUND RD. P.O. BOX 13819 MILWAUKEE, WI 53213

Edited by
Ferdinand David
Revised by
Henry Schradieck

Concerto № 23.

G. B. VIOTTI

✠ vı - - - ae ✠ means, that passages between these signs may be omitted

4

Concerto № 23.

Explanation of the signs.

⊓ Down-bow.
Ⅴ Up-bow.
I E-string.
II A-string.
III D-string.

IV = G-string.
nut = at the nut.
pt. = at the point.
fb. = full-bow.
hb. = half-bow.

mb. = in the middle of the bow.
sh. = short stroke.
br. = broad stroke.

Edited by
Ferdinand David.

Revised by
Henry Schradieck.

Violin.

G. B. VIOTTI.

⊕ vi--de ⊕ means, that passages between these signs may be omitted.

Violin.

Violin.

Violin.

Violin.

Violin.

Violin.

Violin.

Violin.

Violin.

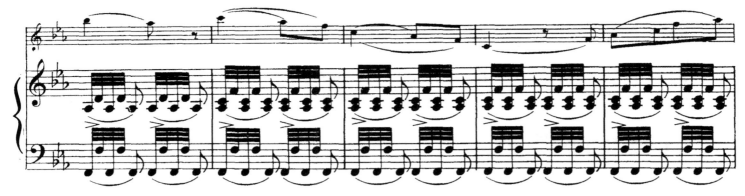